THIS IS THE LAST CALL TO BE SAVED

Table of Contents

CHAPTER 1- Lifestyle of living

Many people, today, live a lifestyle in which there is always "another day" – or what you don't do today, you can always "do tomorrow." Most individuals put this into practice on a daily basis. Since the beginning of man fall, time has been a big issue to grapple with, here on earth. When Jesus steps out of Eternity to come here on Earth, His purpose was to save mankind. As the days continually worsen and become more stressful, people tend to relax and entertain themselves with certain evil events – not realizing they can be a victim next of a tragedy.

When the opportunity to go the Church comes up in a conversation, many use excuse after excuse why not to go. People have tried all kinds of things to correct or better themselves in life; not having Jesus in their style of living unless as a last resort, perhaps never even seeing him as ever being someone who could rescue them from all of the problems they face every day.

When I minister to people about going to church, I have heard several things like, "I have to get myself together before I go," or, "But the game is coming on;" if they are not happy with their lives, perhaps, "I have done too many wicked things and God won't forgive me, I just don't have time to go." (And from those who have forgotten Him, there is a hint of regret, like, "at one time I used to go, but I am not ready right now – I work doing the week, so that's my rest day, and I catch up on my sleep then.")

There are also the dismissive attitudes that come from not having known a good church home and supportive congregation of believers, to share in fellowship with "It's just boring – and I have nothing to wear," or, "I am going to go one day or get back into it, I know people who go to church and do as much dirt as me." When it comes time to the season of giving, the livelihood of a church being at stake – with mounting costs on top of a desire to reach out and serve populations - you could hear those who have not yet seen the value of this as dismissing these missions by declaring, "All those preachers want is your money, remember this God will judge them if they are misusing it." (And the list can keep going on because the word here I am using in this detail always referred with an excuse.)

But the true question is this, "What are you living for?" When this temporal life ends, it shall all fall back into your hands, what you did here on Earth. Many people *never* look at the future of things in their everyday living it always what happening now. And their past can, at times, come back to haunt them. When God has given unto us exceedingly great and precious promises, a person become what they are in life is because of what is in their heart – for as a man thinks in his heart, so is he (Proverbs 23:7, KJV)

Our understanding of this phrase comes from seeing that things in one's heart cause Man either to walk with God or turn from His ways; for example, when I got born again, I asked the Lord to help me out. But, before I received salvation, my wild lifestyle kept me on the streets, living as if there was no tomorrow – in other words, "living life to the fullest."

I used to tell myself, all of the time, "you only live once in life." But what I thought was fun, was sin in the sight of God, because I was looking for love, peace, and answers, in *all* of the wrong places. One of the worst things I would not have wanted to happen to me is to ever experience dying one day, and not being born again. My life needed a change, a big turnaround – not for a moment, but something that would stay with me for the rest of my life – to prevent me from finding myself spending eternity in the lake of fire, somewhere I would regret forever. I needed something to happen right away.

One day, I noticed the changes in a guy I use to work with, seeing how Jesus turned his life around for the better. He had had a strong substance abuse addiction, had gone to church and become saved, and now had a new purpose in life. He got my attention by talking to me, and praying for me, showing me Scriptures in the Bible describing God's greatness and the plan He has for His people. (He even had me to repent, like many people do today – but it was not from my heart they just were empty words coming from my mouth.)

I fought with change for months; I was constantly saying, following the Lord will be taking away all my fun – before I realized that He was adding fun to my life, and showing me how to do this in a righteous way.

One night I rose up with a loud voice and said, "Enough is enough! I am tired of living like this, I no longer want to be a part of this world. All I want is you, Lord! I repent of all my sin." The next thing that happened was a big ball of light that came through the wall, upon my body. It came over me like a rushing mighty wind and it filled me with the Holy Ghost. I then began to speak in other tongues, as the Spirit gave me the utterance.

At the time, I did not belong to any one church – drifting among church homes, constantly visiting but not yet sure where to lay down my roots.

Now, something in the inside had changed – and I became a new man. Indeed, as we are told in the Scripture, "Therefore, if any man be in Christ, he is a new creature: old things are passed away; behold, all things are become new." (2-Corinthians 5:17, KJV). And what I thought what was impossible to do at a time, now became possible for me (Mark 9:23, KJV).

I used be led by what felt good to me, by walking in the flesh. It was a strong hold on my life, that which I enjoyed but was really holding me down and keeping me in darkness – and, after this revelation, what I thought was going to be hard now became easy. I was spiritually blind, at first – but now, I could see.

John, 3:17-21 states,

"For God sent not His son into the world to condemn the world; but that the world through Him might be saved. He that believeth on Him is not condemned: but he that believe not is condemned already; because he hath not believed in the name of the only begotten Son of God. And this is the condemnation that light is come into the world, and men loved darkness rather than light, because their deeds were evil. For everyone that doeth evil hate light neither come to the light, lest his deeds should be reproved. But he that doeth truth come to the light, that his deeds maybe made manifest that they are wrought in God" (John 3:17-21, KJV).

Now, the long fight was over; the devil lost another soul.

I, myself, used to struggle in my walk with the Lord, for a while, before I gave up the fight for the better – and not for the worst.

Jesus states, in Luke 15:10, "Likewise, I say unto you, there is joy in the presence of the angels of God over one sinner that repenteth" (KJV). I understood this and the idea that I could not come to Christ without my mind being renewed, as He had given me a new way of thinking, spiritually – because the old way of thinking had passed with my salvation.

My mind was refreshed, as now, I had the mind of Christ – I recognized this much in my past; I learned a lot to my own understanding, and did things in my strength.

As a preacher, I see that that many people are lost, today, and are unaware of it; on the other hand, there are also a great many people who are struggling and dealing with the right decision to daily surrender and give it up to the Lord.

As Scripture tells us, our life and death's sentence is in the power of our tongue. In Proverbs 18:21, we are told, "The Lord did something for me and it still remains today in my walk. He never left me, nor forsakes me" (Prov. 18:21, KJV). In times of trouble, many Christians have given the things of God up through bad trials, by not getting the victory.

When the door of opportunity is opened, many Christians have stopped at the entrance and looked back – instead of going forth, to fulfill the calling of God's purpose, in their life.

A lot of Christians are waiting on God; in reality, God is waiting for them.

When coming over to Christ, God see us as overcomers – and nothing less.

There are times when your flesh gets weak and you feel the weight of so many obstacles piling up. This is not the time to turn your back on God, but the hour has to rise up and say it, like you *mean* it, "The battle is not mine but it's the Lord's".

In doing this, we recognize that, while problems can be against you – and you feel like your back can be against the wall – but God is there for you, to answer every problem you face.

So many men and women are saying, it is just too hard to serve the Lord, in this modern era. When you give the world too much influence over your life, you build up spiritual walls in your style of living, and so many things fall back to hurt you – but, when you confess, it easy to walk with Christ, and you can see that it is because the spiritual walls surrounding you have been destroyed.

Philippians 4:13 tells us, "I can do all things through Christ which strengthen me" (Phil. 4:12, KJV) and it is just that easy, when you allow Jesus to be a part of your entire existence – because He lives *inside* of you, as you find yourself continually questioning why you hang onto sinful things which are not pleasing in the sight of God.

By the same token, in 2-Corinthians 4:18, Paul states, "While we look not at the things which are seen, but at the things which are seen are temporal; but the things which are not seen are eternal" (2 Cor. 4:18, KJV). This Scripture is telling us that the life we live in our body, on Earth, is but temporal living – meaning that, as men, women, and children, you don't have to go through the worst of the worst.

For it ended once you turned your life toward Jesus – and you can start again, immediately, if you cast these burdens aside, stop running from God.

...And, instead, run to Him.

CHAPTER 2- Spirits in Hell are crying out

This sinful world offers so many things – but Jesus offers so much more, whether you believe it or not. People die every day, not having a relationship with Jesus as their Lord and Savior – and they spend the remainder of their spiritual lives in a place called Hell.

Many say this is Hell, here on Earth; they are referring to the nature by which a person lives, day by day – but this Hell, which I am talking about, is the spiritual places where a person's spirit goes to receive torment by the devil; sadly, many will not believe it, until they go to this place.

Spirits are crying out in torment, right now, as you read this book – because they want another chance, they made their final decision here on Earth. I write this not to scare you or to frighten you, but to warn you of what might happen to someone if they continue to resist the Lord and what the Bible and its teachings hold to be true.

Jesus presents us with a story of two men who live here on Earth – and, one day, both die and when to, two different places – in Luke, 16:20-31:

"And there was a certain beggar named Lazarus which was laid at his gate, full of sores, and desiring to be fed with the crumbs which fell from the rich man's table; moreover the dogs came and licked his sores. And it came to pass, that the beggar died, and was carried by the angels into Abrahams bosom. The rich man also died, and was buried; and in Hell he lift up his eyes, being in torments and seeth Abraham afar off, and Lazarus in his bosom. And cried and said, 'Father Abraham, have mercy on me, and send Lazarus, that he may dip the tip of his finger in water, and cool my tongue; for I am tormented in this flame.'
"But Abraham said, 'Son, remember that thou in thy lifetime receivedst thy good things and likewise Lazarus evil things: but now he is comforted, and thou art tormented. And beside all this, between us and you there is a great gulf fixed: so that they which would pass from hence to you cannot; neither can they pass to us, that would come from thence.'
"Then he said, 'I pray thee therefore, Father, that thou wouldest send him to my father's house: For I have five brethren; that he may testify unto them, lest they also come into this place of torment.'
"Abraham saith unto him, "They have Moses and the prophet; let them hear them."
"And he said, 'Nay, Father Abraham: but if one went unto them from the dead, they will repent.'
"And He said unto him, 'If they hear not Moses and the prophets, neither will they be persuaded, though one rose from the dead.'" (Luke, 16:20-31, KJV).
The ones that are there in Hell wish they had your opportunity – and, since you still have it, right now, they want you to know that the choice is real.
Jesus explains how to receive this gift (and Him) in Matthew 10:39: "He that findeth his life shall lose it and he that lose his life for my sake shall find it" (Mat. 10:39, KJV) telling us that we must give up our sinful ways of living and receive Jesus and God's way of doing things. For God is not only using this book to win souls to His kingdom; if you look around your neighborhood or where you are, right now, Jesus is broadcasting around the world *every day* for someone like you – yet, because of disobedience, lack of understanding, and our blindness to recognizing that Jesus Christ is the son of God, He remains seated in heaven on the right hand of the Father.
Jesus came here just for you, don't pass up this golden opportunity.

In life, a person can ignore or regret certain things that come by their way – and if we wait too long, we will live in regret, as the rich man did in this parable, knowing that we could have had this salvation, if we had only made the attempt.

Receiving salvation is greater than all gifts, for this is where you decide where you want to spend eternity at.

One Sunday, I was preaching the Word – and, after the service was over, I called souls up to be born again, when a man pulled me over to the side, and told me, "My parents took care of my salvation when I was a baby."

I told him that I understood what he was saying, to show respect for his experiences – but asked if I could share with him what Jesus said about how to receive Him.

He accepted, and I then opened my Bible to Roman 10:9-10, which states,

"That if thou shall confess with thy mouth the Lord Jesus and shalt believe in thine heart that God hath raised him from the dead, thou shalt be saved. For with the heart man believeth unto righteousness; and with the mouth confession is made unto salvation" (Rom. 10:9-10, KJV).

A baby first has to learn how to talk and believe that Jesus is the way to their salvation; after they accept it as part of their life, then this passage (above) is ready to be activated in their life for salvation.

Like them, we need to stop letting things or misled errors talk you out to receive salvation, scriptures teach and correct the believer how to receive salvation and there is no other way – because the enemy is trying his best to take as many souls as possible along with him, and further away from God. It is important not to let yourself be the next victim, even if you are not sure where you may spend the rest of your life at, for here is your golden chance. For one day, you will go to be with the Lord – and you be glad you received salvation. And you know one thing, already – which is that the enemy wasn't able to talk you out of it.

People are dying *every* day, without salvation – and then, they realize that Jesus is real. And that everything which was said about Him, and they are wishing they were still in your footsteps. For the Word of God is *warning* people.

Adam was the first man on earth to be warned.

God made a covenant with him, and commanded him not to eat of the Tree of Knowledge of good and evil; in so doing, God showed him the *very* thing what would be the cause of that which is death, today.

Right now, today, God is *warning* mankind about receiving Jesus as their Lord and Savior, to avoid. Remember Luke 13:23-30:

"Then said one unto him, 'Lord, are there few that be saved?' And He said unto them, 'Strive to enter in at the strait gate: for many, I say unto you, will seek to enter in, and shall not be able. When once the master of the house is risen up, and hath shut to the door, and ye begin to stand without, and to knock at the door, saying, Lord, Lord, open unto us; and he shall answer and say unto you, I know you not whence ye are: Then shall ye begin to say, "We have eaten and drunk in thy presence, and thou hast taught in our streets." But he shall say, "I tell you, I know you not whence ye are; depart from me, all ye workers of iniquity." There shall be weeping and gnashing of teeth, when ye shall see Abraham, and Isaac, and Jacob, and all of the prophets, in the kingdom of God, and you yourselves thrust out. And they shall come from the East, and from the West, and from the North, and from the South, and shall sit down in the kingdom of God. And, behold, there are last which shall be first, and there are first which shall be last'" (Luke 13:23-30, KJV).

CHAPTER 3 - YOUR RELIGION CAN'T SAVE YOU

Across many different religious beliefs, in their practice of serving God, many people think they are the only chosen ones going to Heaven, or to this new Earth, which God has prepared for them – and anyone who is not part of their belief is unsaved, or even *infidel*.

Even among their own community, in some religious sects, they still feel that the devil has caused confession to many, regardless of where their fellowship is at. By their superficial judgment, seeing only the surface of people and their experiences, they are quick to judge who is going to be accepted into Heaven and who will not be going there. In other words, they can determine through works who is saved and the ones who are not saved. (Remember the custom of the scribes who were teachers of the law, who looked at Jesus from the outside *according to the flesh* and judged Him as not being the Christ.)

Jesus states, in Matthew 7: 1-2: "Judge not that ye be not judged. For with what judgment ye shall be judged: and with what measure ye mete, it shall be measured to you again" (Mat. 7:1-2, KJV).

One day, my wife and I were coming home from a hospital, when we saw a woman who was stranded outside the building and needed a ride home. We offered her a ride to her destination, and, as we were taking her home, Jesus came up in our conversation. The lady said she was saved, sanctified, and filled with the Holy Ghost. She told us what religion she belonged to; I then asked her, "In which religion do you have to belong to, in order to be saved by someone?" The woman said, "If you are not of my religion, you are not saved." I then asked her to show me, in the Bible, where I am required to be part of her belief system, to be saved and be welcomed into Heaven.

She did not have an answer, because it was not in there.

In Galatians 2: 16-21, Paul writes:

"Knowing that a man is not justified by the works of the law, but by the faith of Jesus Christ, even we have believed in Jesus Christ, that we might be justified by the faith of Christ, and not by the works of the law: for by the works of the law shall no flesh be justified. But if, while we seek to be justified by Christ, we ourselves also are found sinners, is therefore Christ the minister of sin? God forbid. For if I build again the things which I destroyed, I make myself a transgressor. For I through the law am dead to the law, that I might live unto God. I am crucified with Christ: never the less I live; yet not I, but Christ liveth in me: and the life which I now live in the flesh I live by the faith of the Son of God, who loved me, and gave himself for me. I do not frustrate the grace of God: for if righteousness come by the law, then Christ is dead in vain" (Gal. 2:6-12, KJV).

Now, God has justified the believers, for He has made us righteous – not by a man religion traditions ways, whereby using the tool of God to act upon what they believe in what is righteous, with their path become carnal. He has told us that righteousness starts with Jesus, and ends with Him. For Jesus is the only one who can save us – not by works, if by works was what was said by Jesus, in vain – but by grace, as the believer lives through faith in Jesus and in their walk with Him.

As the Scripture says, the just shall live, by faith and not by a manmade religion, come to know Him. In 1-John 3:1-3, the apostle John declares:

"Behold, what manner of love the Father hath bestowed upon us, that we should be called the sons of God therefore the world knoweth us not, because it knew him not. Beloved now are we the sons of God, and it doth not yet appear what we shall be: but we know that, when he shall appear, we shall be like him for we shall see him as he is. Every man that hath this hope in him purifieth himself, even as he is pure" (1 John 3:1-3 KJV).

What this passage tells us is that we should not have known names – or, in other words name yourself after a sect or denomination, to set yourself apart from others – for many who follow other faiths are quick to say what religion they are, but Jesus came down from Heaven so that all who follow Him would all be one, and be a unified church body, without the religious names that prevent us from fellowshipping with one another.

The Word of God instructs us to be one in *unity*, as, in Psalm 133:1, which instructs, "Behold, how good and how pleasant it is for brethren to dwell together in unity" (Ps. 133:1, KJV).

Jesus, Himself, speaks to people who thought they were righteous because they used His name in their works, as he explains to them (in Matthew 7:21-23):

"Not everyone that saith unto me, 'Lord, Lord,' shall enter into the kingdom of heaven; but he that doeth the will of my Father which is in heaven. Many will say to me in that day, Lord, Lord, have we not prophesied in thy name? and in thy name have cast out devils? And in thy name done many wonderful works? and then will I profess unto them, I never knew you: depart from me, ye that, work iniquity" (Mat. 7:21-23, KJV).

That is a powerful statement, by which Scripture teaches us that we must be born again, so that we can know the will of the Father, who is in heaven – and be separated from the iniquities which guide some people, and keep them believing that they are doing what is right in the sight of God through works alone, whereby Jesus will not come to know them. For, when you are born of God he knows you, because God has created righteousness, not mankind; when you know Him and He knows you, then His ways come in your heart.

If you do not come to know Him through Jesus, then the operation of the flesh leads you – and mankind will guide you into error. Another thing to remember is that, without the Spirit of Truth which guides you into all truths, no one knows the meaning of what the truth is all about (John 16:13). KJV

CHAPTER 4 - GOD WARNS HIS PEOPLE

Jesus speaks through Scripture. Be not deceived, Paul says, because the world is full of traps and doom days: "Finally, my brethren, be strong in the Lord, and in the power of his might. Put on the whole armour of God,that ye may be able to stand against the wiles of the devil." (Ephs 6:10-11, KJV).

When a person is deceived, it is because of not being aware of the consequences, for many are falling simply for what sounds good in a hedonistic way. Remember how sin started, in the Garden of Eden, with the Tree of Knowledge (of good and evil) in the beginning days of Mankind, with Adam and Eve – when, one day, while walking through the Garden by the Tree of Knowledge, Adam and Eve experienced temptation whereby the serpent in the garden persuaded Eve in eating off the tree which God forbidding them to eat from. Even though she ate from the fruit of the tree, she said she knew what was right to the serpent (which was *not* to eat from the tree) – but her action of not doing what was told led her and Adam into error:

"Genesis 3:6: And when the woman saw that the tree was good for food and that it was pleasant to the eyes, and a tree to be desired to make one wise, she took of the fruit thereof, and did eat, and gave also unto her husband with her; and he did eat." (Gen. 3:6, KJV)
And from that point on, when forced to make decisions between what's right and wrong, in matters that force us to deal with good and evil, the gate of knowledge is left wide open for mankind. Violence is so common, today, that when something bad happens, people no longer react to it – it's impossible to avoid in the news, our neighborhoods, and the cartoon characters and games marketed to us for our children.

In 2-Timothy 3:1-5, Paul writes:

"This know also, that in the last days perilous times shall come. For men shall be lovers of their own selves, covetous, boasters, proud, blasphemers, disobedient to parents, unthankful, unholy, without natural affection, trucebreakers, false accusers, incontinent, fierce, despisers of those that are good, traitor, heady, highminded, lovers of pleasures more than lovers of God; having a form of godliness, but denying the power thereof: from such turn away. Right now threw out the world you see the acts of these five verse go through the face of the earth in a disaster way." (2 Tim. 3:1-5, KJV)
Similarly, in Matthew, Chapter 24, Jesus warns the believer about the up-and-coming things that shall happen, a big key to the future – for He says to take heed, that no man should deceive you. Jesus mentions the false Christs who come in his name, meaning people who are part of religious groups or organization are not always aware of being deceived by what they practice and believe in, within these bodies – be it false prophets, rumors of wars, nations against nations, kingdoms against kingdoms, famines, diseases, earthquakes in diverse places, and many other things are you ready and prepared when all these things come to pass.

When you are *born again,* walking in God's righteousness not only prepares you, it protects you. It doesn't take a rocket science to see what's happening every day, in our society, to lead us closer away from God and his plan for us and into the destruction of mankind.

If you never ask if you are in the right place, you will never know.

The clock is ticking to get born, again – and see the things of God clearly.

CHAPTER 5 - DON'T FALL AWAY

When believers whom walk with God fall away, it is because while – even though, in the beginning of their walk with God, the excitement was first there and it looked as if nothing could go wrong – for all was good with the word of God and it had a strong influence on their lives – they were thrown by the trials that came next. They succumbed to the hard surroundings in their path: temptations, weakness, sickness, relationship, money and a host of other problems.

Even when these are just the ordinarily difficult trials which flare up in daily life without struggles, the pressures they face – day in and day out -make it look like there is no growth or change. One thing after another keeps accruing, and they can't withstand it any longer. The promises made are taken too literally, like "many mansions" and being made "fishers of men," without probing to see the deeper wisdom and knowledge that is readily available, and the peace that having a stronger relationship with the Lord could bring to their lives.

The "easy way out," for them, is then to give up - because nothing seems like it is working out for them, with only hard times in their way; indeed, when people have told me why they stopped going to church, they said, "I thought, if I leave God, things will get better – and the peer pressure of the world won't be there anymore, trying to lead me away."

However, if they stopped and listened, they would see that the right path can be found if they attend the word of God:

"Turn, O backsliding children, saith the Lord; for I am married unto you: and I will take you one of a city, and two of a family, and I will bring you to Zion: And I will give you pastors according to mine heart, which shall feed you with knowledge and understanding" (Jer. 3:14-15, KJV).
Scripture reminds us that having struggles and difficulties in life is a set-up, meant to cause believers to fall away from the Word. Like an enemy, pushing them to test their strength and ability to do the right thing.

In the book of Job, we hear mention about his life going so well, and have descriptions of his blessings and vast material wealth.

Then, one day, the devil put it upon himself to thrust Job into a series of harsh trials, meant to get him to give up and turn away from God. Despite the losses of his wealth and family, he never gave up on his faith. With patience and perseverance, Job's relationship and obedience to God stayed the same, as he overcame this fall; he was rewarded for his faithfulness, in the end, when he saw all he had lost return to him, with God increasing his wealth multifold.

Remember that Jesus endured similar trials when he was in the wilderness; his ability to withstand gives us an even stronger example of what to do in times of trouble. This episode, mentioned in Luke 4:1-4, shows him going through many of the same stages that we, as believers, go through when we are tempted by the world:

"And Jesus being full of the Holy Ghost returned from Jordan and was led by the Spirit into the wilderness, being forty days tempted of the devil. And in those days he did eat nothing: and when they were ended, he afterward hungered. And the devil said unto him, if thou be the Son of God, command this stone that it be made bread. And Jesus answered him saying, it is written, that man shall not live by bread alone, but by every word of God." (Luke 4:1-4, KJV)

Jesus here made a key point in remaining faithful to God's will, in showing that a believer must speak the word of God, no matter how it may sound or come across to others – because, as you overcome your trials, your faith to withstand them becomes your testimony of His blessings in your life, as you recognize your victory from trusting the word of God throughout.

There is nothing out there which can outdo or stand up against it.

Hebrews 4:12 states, "For the word of God is quick, and sharper than any two-edged sword, piercing even to the dividing asunder of soul and spirit, and is a discerner of the thoughts and intents of the heart."

How many out there have giving up or left the church because of being offended, bitterness or some kind of other reason for the word, "sake"? Jesus explains about the fall of many over the word of God and also those who reap on good ground using the word let's look very close about the saying of the sower in Mark 4:10-20:

"And when he was alone, they that were about him with the twelve asked of him the parable. Jesus said unto them, 'Unto you it is given to know the mystery of the kingdom of God: but unto them that are without, all these things are done in parables: That seeing they may see, and not perceive; and hearing they may hear, and not understand; lest at any time they should be converted, and their sins should be forgiven them.' And he said unto them, 'Know you not this parable? And how then will you know all parables? The sower soweth the word. And these are they by the way side, where the word is sown; but when they have heard, Satan cometh immediately, and taketh away the word that was sown in their hearts. And these are they likewise which are sown on stony ground; who, when they have heard the word, immediately receive it with gladness: And have no root in themselves, and so endure but for a time: afterward, when affliction or persecution ariseth for the word's sake, immediately they are offended. And these are they which are sown among thorns such as hear the word, And the cares of this world, and the deceitfulness of riches, and the lusts of other things entering in choke the word, and it becometh unfruitful. And these are they which are sown on good ground; such as hear the word and receive it, and bring forth fruit some thirtyfold, some sixtyfold, and some an hundred.'" (Mark 4:10-20, KJV)

Here, Jesus talks about four different types of people, three of whom did not see the fruit of the word produced in their life; the group which *did* remain faithful, saw the manifestation of the word stand firm, and here you can clearly see the blessing of the Lord.

CHAPTER 6 – A TRUE WITNESS

God has called those whom are born of Him, or "born again," to be a true witness, here on Earth.

In this natural world, when a crime takes place, the police force is always looking for more evidence; they actively pursue witnesses who saw the truth of what happened and can help them put together the pieces and bring the perpetrator to justice.

Spiritually, the situation remains the same, when God sends forth his true witness – someone whom has spiritual proof and shows evidence of their faith in God in their walk, as they bear testimony to the acts of God from living in grace.

Throughout the Bible, God calls upon His prophets and people to be a witness to Him and the Kingdom of God, for the nonbelievers. Before the first church even organized, in the book of Acts, Jesus reminds them of that which is proven in Chapter One of Acts, which is to wait for the promise of the Father: "But you shall receive power, after that the Holy Ghost is come upon you: and you shall be witnesses unto me in both in Jerusalem, and in all Judaea, and in Samaria, and unto the uttermost part of the earth" (Acts 1:8, KJV).

Once the Holy Spirit came up on them, the witnesses of Jesus were told not to stay and preach the Gospel only within their communities, but to go forth throughout the Earth.

Chapter Five of the first Book of John talks about the importance of the commandment to be witness of God to our fellow men. I John 5:9 states, "If we receive the witness of men, the witness Of God is greater: for this is the witness of God which he hath testified of his son." This continues with the next verse (I John 5:10), which tells us, "He that believeth on the Son of God hath the witness in himself: he that believeth not God hath made him a liar; because he believeth not the record that God gave of his Son."

Jesus's disciples bore witness to the many wonderful things He did, as recorded in the Word of God. With this, they also gave their testimony to their own experiences during their time with Him, because he lived in them as born-again *believers*. False witnesses are put into our path, as Christians, to try and deceive those who are unaware of the Truth – those who are not as close in their walk to still give the world some influence, which makes them susceptible to those that would fool or trick them.

Proverbs 12:17 instructs, "He that speaketh truth showeth forth righteousness: but a false witness deceit. Him that the Lord send to witness spread the good news" (Prov. 12:17, KJV).

Similarly, in Proverbs 14:25, we are told, "A true witness delivereth souls: but a deceitful witness speaketh lies" (Prov. 14:25, KJV).

Witnesses in the Old Testament

God called upon Abraham to be a father of many nations and the material blessings from that contract with God can still be witnessed today.

God called Moses and Aaron to bear witness to him as they prepared to go into Egypt to deliver the people from the Egyptian. People can believe a truth or a lie, without ever having seen it or heard it; needing the truth, Moses sent twelve spies to check out the land of Canaan.

Ten of the men who witnessed it then returned to him and told him, Aaron, and the congregation of the children of Israel, the people were stirred up by this report, in Numbers 13:32-33:

"And they brought up an evil report of the land which they had searched unto the children of Israel, saying, the land, through which we have gone to search it, is a land that eateth up the inhabitants thereof; and all the people that we saw in it are men of a great stature. And there we saw the giant, the sons of Anak, which come of the giants: and we were in our own sight as grasshoppers, and so we were in their sight" (Num. 13:32-33, KVJ)
After this was said about the land in Number 14:1 states, "And all the congregation lifted up their voice, and cried; and the people wept that night."

Now, when the children of Israel heard this, what moved them was only this second-hand account; they had not yet seen the giants or the land for themselves, and just believed it to be an insurmountable obstacle to their freedom. This triggered murmuring and dissention, as they started pointing fingers and blaming Moses, Aaron, and their promises of God's will; they could not see, for their weaknesses, that God was bigger or mightier than the people. (Indeed, if we do not recognize His greatness and blessings to us, any difficult task or temptation seems impossible.)

The other two members of that party, Caleb and Joshua, saw it differently, however –and were bold enough to share that separate vision with the people.

When they visited Canaan, they saw immediately that it could be possessed – much as in the modern era, when we see that our political leaders talk a good game plan, filled with campaign "promises" and prompts to action, but then fade back when challenges and a righteous path seem too hard to stand by. By contrast, God always raises up strong leaders, no matter what their background is – for he examines our hearts and knows that our spirit is what is important, not the outside appearance which man can see.

On the importance of being a true witness

Remember that the apostle, Paul, when his name was still Saul (before his conversion to the Lord) bore false witness against the church, at that time when there was a great persecution against the church which was congregated at Jerusalem.

Saul was, originally, very much against Jesus – but, as he was going to Damascus, as recounted in the book of Acts, all of this changed all this changed:

"And as he journeyed, he came near Damascus: and suddenly there shined round about him a light from heaven: As he fell to the earth, and heard a voice saying unto him, Saul, Saul, why persecutes thou me?

And he said, who art thou, Lord? And the Lord said, I am Jesus whom thou persecutes: it is hard for thee to kick against the pricks" (Acts 9:3-5, KJV).
When this happened, Saul's heart changed and he became a passionate follower of Jesus – recognizing the Lord's calling and becoming a true witness of God. Even as believers, we still remember a time when we had false ideas about this religion – but, after we witnessed the Lord's greatness, submitted ourselves to the truth and what a walk with Him really meant.

The Call to Action

In the Book of Revelation, Chapter 11 talks about two witnesses who were sent by God; verses 3-4 state: "And I will give power unto my two witnesses, and they shall prophesy a thousand two hundred and threescore days clothed in sackcloth. These are the two olive trees, and the two candlesticks standing before the God of the earth" (Rev. 11:3-4, KVJ).

Only when the Lord calls upon you can you be considered a true witness. For, as we are instructed, Jesus's sheep hear His voice and a stranger they will not follow, as in John 10:1-5:

"'Verily, verily, I say unto you, He that entereth not by the door into the sheepfold, but climbeth up some other way, the same is a thief and a robber. But he that entereth in by the door is the shepherd of the sheep. To him the porter openeth; and the sheep hear his voice: and he calleth his own sheep by name, and leadeth them out. And when he putteth forth his own sheep, he goeth before them, and the sheep follow him: for they know his voice. And a stranger will they not follow, but will flee from him: for they know not the voice of strangers'" (John 10:1-5, KJV).
(Remember: Jesus was our "true witness", sent from above, to lead us into all righteousness.)

I can testify to this in my own life, recalling an episode from my early teens when I was coming home from the park and a man in a green suit came up to me and asked me, "Do you believe that Jesus is the Son of God?" and I said, "Yes." He then prayed for me and continued on his way; when he spoke, my memory of his conviction told me how strong a true witness's commitment to sharing the word of of God can be as he seeks to help and strengthen others.

CHAPTER 7 - THERE IS A REAL GOD

For all the atheism who does not believe there is not a God, a spiritual blindness of unawareness is in their path. Look around you everything which is seen or not been seen is created by God, that mean there is a maker which has a beginning and a ending for all things, there is a birth which is a start too everything that been made there's no way by it or threw it since the creation of God. All things will know there is a true God, whether they live to see it or die to see it, as shown in John 1:1-4:

"In the beginning was the Word, and the Word was with God, and the Word was God. The same was in the beginning with God. All things were made by him; and without him was not anything made that was made. In him was life; and the life was the light of men" (John 1:1-4, KJV)s.
The phrase, "All things are by Him," means that everything were created for His pleasure and fulfillment, regardless of whether or not we understand how – for God will make Himself known, and, when that day comes, every knee shall bow and every tongue shall confess that Jesus is Lord. This means that, as believers, we must bow to our knees, as well, continuing to show our faith in His righteousness and protection.

There will be no room for excuses like those someone here on Earth might make, for to have faith in God means his will must be done.

People may say, on this Day of Judgment, "I did not know if God still even existed, because of all the turmoil, the violence, the evil acts and the natures of problems happening so often in our society – which made it seem like it was not a God around. However, if you can accept that believing in Him is, in itself, a powerful tool – for, indeed, everything is recorded and nothing is without excuse – you will find grace in knowing that the only way out of this is not just believing there is a God, but also believing in His son Jesus for eternal life, and this belief will set you apart from those who deny him as our days worsen and we near the events outlined in the Book of Revelation.

When a person doesn't believe in God, this belief is called "unbelief" – and, until a person is born again, *he or she cannot see the kingdom of God.*

What this means is that there are two births which must take place: emerging from our mother's womb and being born again as believers. The first one, when a baby comes into the world, is being *born of the flesh*. Being such, they are of the flesh –and, as they grow up and live in this nature (as mankind was born into sin and did not know the right ways of God) they are perpetually lost on this earth, unless they are converted to believers in Him. For this to happen, a *second* birth must take place. When that happens, we are born of the Spirit of Christ – and that which is born of the Spirit is Spirit; our souls are born again within our bodies and we have the nature of the real God living within us. (This baptism symbolizes a spiritual birth taking place in their life, and that person is *born again* of God – enabling them to see and understand His kingdom and vision for us.)

Scripture describes the importance of being *born again* in John 3:5:

> "Jesus answered, 'Verily, verily, I say unto you, except a man be born of water and of the Spirit, he cannot enter into the kingdom of God" (John 3:5, KJV).

This is a very powerful statement, for it tells us that God is speaking *continuously* through us, as believers, showing that he exists.

As far as the existence of God, Himself, is concerned, we can consider the fact that He does not have a birthday – because he was never *born*. Instead of thereby tracing his origins or lineage, we can and should accept that God has always been here; He is eternal, and not constricted by time, as is Man, because of the Fall of Man – which happened when God's first creation, Adam, disobeyed him, resulting in mankind leaving the eternity of the Garden of Eden and going to a state in which he felt sin and death. (And has been needing a Savior – because so many of us are still lost, here on Earth.)

In the Bible – which is the Word of God, recorded for us to study and use as a manual, to help us, the human race, understand him – the Lord speaks about how all things are created by Him and through him, in Isaiah 45:5-7:
"I am the Lord, and there is none else, there is no God beside me: I girded thee, though thou hast not known me. That they may know from the rising of the sun, and from the west, that there is none beside me. I am the Lord, and there is none else. I form the light, and create darkness: I make peace, and create evil: I the Lord do all these things. God is in the heavens: he hath done whatsoever he hath pleased" (Is. 45:5-7, KJV).
God is not like some idols, which are manmade or an object we have chosen to worship; God is, instead, a spirit – and those who worship Him must worship Him in spirit and in truth. People who are not yet believers may ask you questions like, "How can when you do not, you pray to someone you cannot even see?" The idea of it may not make sense to the *natural man,* who doesn't believe there is a God:

"But the natural man receiveth not the things of the Spirit of God: for they are foolishness unto him: neither can he know them, because they are spiritually discerned. But he that is spiritual judgeth all things, yet he himself is judged of no man. For who hath known the mind of the Lord, that he may instruct him? But we have the mind of Christ" (I Cor. 2:14-16, KJV).
Once an atheist has converted, and gone through these stages, they too, though, will come to recognize that there is a real God – as they, themselves, can now see Him and His guidance in their life. Until that happens, it is important not to let their disbelief and pressuring sway our own faith in Him.

> *When a true believer is connected with God, His Spirit dwells within their body, a presence which they then worship as a spirit.*

Another thing which keeps people in unbelief about whether or not there is a God, are the spiritual forces which prevent you from recognizing what is happening in your life. These forces will continue to keep people from seeing God, because they are part of a demonic system which is meant to keep people blind and unlearned from knowing the true God.

It is true that His ways of doing things are totally different from those of mankind. When learning about God it's not like man's education system, for the knowledge of God is spiritual and comes from above – and we must, therefore, be born of Him in order to understand His ways of doing. Those who are not yet able to receive Him fall susceptible to confusion, unbelief, and foolish earthly reasoning (or false logic) as to why you God must not be real, because they do not yet allow themselves to know Him and trust in His greater plan and the blessings meant for us.

All of mankind exercises free will; making choices in one's life plays a big part. It is important to realize that our actions start with us and end by what we have chosen to do, here on Earth. When I talk about the Lord Jesus Christ and His influence on my life, I tell others of how real He is and how He has revealed himself to me, supernaturally – beginning with my first memory of Him, at age five, and even today, when I still witness supernatural things.

As we make these decisions, it is important to remember that God loves us, and has called upon true witnesses and those around you to speak of Him – including myself as I write this book.

He is waiting on you, wanting a relationship with you – so, why time waiting to get to know Him for the very last breath that you may take, instead of enjoying His blessings, immediately?

Have you ever heard someone say I told you so here is your moment? You have so many people don't believe in anything until the very thing which was said come to pass. Don't forget these words I told you so and many other people who have said it to you, through television, computers, devices, radio, books, magazines – and their own testimonies. Those who are still non-believers may say that, once you die, there is no after-life. But they are lying, for the reality is that the dead cannot communicate with the living. Which is why, even if someone rose up from the dead to communicate with a non-believer, as Jesus did, they would still not believe – because they are closed off from the truth, which is that, when a person dies, they really will find out how real everything is which was told them about God, in their lifetime, and be wishing for a second chance, as was the rich man who knew Lazarus and, when God denied him entry into heaven for Lazarus, pleaded with God to send Lazarus back to earth to save his family from the same fate. (Luke 16: 19-31)

God of the spirits of all flesh. I lie not when I say that God has reveal His supernatural truths to me – and that I, thereby, speak *only* the truth, as, without the Spirit of Truth, no man or woman knows the full truth of God.

It is important for you to realize, as a believer, that your faith in God and his son, Jesus, is the greatest decision you could ever have made – and that, even with the trials and hardships you will face, His guidance will make it one you will never regret. It is important not to let bitterness creep in, making you like the atheists; if you call upon the almighty God with a repented heart, He will show you great and mighty things to come. For God truly loves you, and He is speaking to you by the words of this book – and many other things in your life which have not yet been recognized as belonging to Him and being part of His grace.

This is the last call for souls, for He is calling out to you, right now, to believe in Him – and it is my prayer (as an author and preacher) for someone like you to be able to hear the word of truth, which is created by the only living God.

CHAPTER 8 - JESUS IS THE SON OF GOD

It is important to note that the Bible is not just a guide, for Christians, but a historic document with events that can be traced to other records of the era – showing that every word which was prophesied by Moses and the other prophets of the Old Testament, about Jesus and his coming as our Messiah – has come to pass, though spoken nearly two thousand years ago. The facts given by the Scripture about His birth, the mighty acts He did among people, the rejection of the people not receiving Him fully as Christ, when He was crucified on the cross, and even his return (leaving the empty tomb.)

Many of the people who knew Jesus, while He walked among them on Earth – Jews and others, alike – could not recognize Him as the Messiah, and were blind to His teachings, even with His warnings. Jesus was indeed the real Christ, the son of God, sent to witness to them – and they missed out on him.

Similarly, there are those, today, who just say that Jesus was only a prophet – and not the son of God. We hear these "religious" people say that we are all sons of God, and that Jesus was merely another human being, and a witness and a great prophet – but not the Messiah. They are setting themselves up for a false Messiah, one who will come to them with false signs and wonders by which they shall be deceived. They will be lured in by the craftiness of witchcraft, and the world shall worship him (this false prophet) and his deceptive words, and this Antichrist – who is only a pretender and not their real Savior – will lead people into chasing after him and receiving his image, as he tries to imitate Jesus. (And I believe his name shall be call Emanuel (but that what I believe) this liar is coming for Jerusalem.)

However, instead of following him to the Kingdom of Heaven – as those who have accepted Jesus and Lord and Savior will, those who follow this false prophet will be set for doomsday (and will not know the truth, until it is too late.)

As believers, even with these false prophets and naysayers trying to convince us otherwise, we need to remember that the truth is in Jesus, the real Christ – who has manifested Himself supernaturally to me and to the rest of us, as the living Son of God. He is the way, the truth, and the life – and no man cometh unto the father, but by Jesus.

In John, Chapter 10:1-2, Jesus tells us that He is the way as he reminds us, "Verily, verily, I say unto you, he that enter not by the door into the sheepfold, but climb up some other way, the same is a thief and a robber. But he that enter in by the door is the Shepherd of the sheep" (John 10:1-2, KJV).

There are many false prophets, even among the Christian faith – who bear witness to a false Christ. Man at times, can be so quick to receive wrong information which feels "easy" to them and makes sense to their natural mind, instead of having to meditate and submit to the will of God –when the true things of God are accepted there can be a different view of things you did not know because of rejecting the truth, the witness of God is far more greater than men. (And, thus, the blind will lead the blind into a ditch.)

Therefore, It is important to remember – and bear witness to others, to save them – that Jesus did not leave his mission of salvation when he departed from Earth; instead, he left the Holy Spirit, which can lead you to all truth – so that no individual could be "set up" by false doctrines and religions which the devil has camped around, here on Earth, the harmful influences and blinders that cannot be recognized by non-believers.

In first book of John, 5:9-13 states:

"If we receive the witness of men, the witness of God is greater: for this is the witness of God which he hath testified of his Son. He that believeth on the Son of God hath the witness of God in himself: he that believeth not God hath made him a liar; because he believeth not the record that God gave of his Son. And this is the record, that God hath given to us eternal life, and this life is in his Son. He that hath the Son hath life; and he that hath not the Son of God hath not life. These things have I written unto you that believe on the name of the Son of God; that you may know that you have eternal life, and that you may believe on the name of the Son of God" (I John 5:9-13, KJV).
Jesus Christ, who came to us as our Messiah, was the real Savior; he who is yet to come, the Antichrist, is the false Messiah, set to deceive the whole world. His influence can already be seen, in how he has already transmitted through his follower's hearts a desire to take over Jerusalem – because his children say that the Holy City belongs to them because, Ishmael was Abraham older son and it belonged to his descendents (his "seeds.")

However, God gave it to Isaac and his seed for the promise was with them – as it yet remains, today and for all eternity.

This false religion's prophet who will come about – their Messiah – will come, and will promise peace, and bring a lot of good things to pass, here on Earth. These "blessings," though, will be brought upon this Earth to deceive mankind – and to cause them to receive a mark on their body, to buy and sell.

This false prophet is coming to change the laws, so those who are deceived by him and his "blessings" shall follow him, instead of Jesus. His time on Earth, as he gathers these lost souls, will be a brief one – and the war, Armageddon, will be set up at Jerusalem *because* of this false leader. The image then worshipped of him will be like that of an idol – and, despite his apparent blessings and gifts to the people, error is before all them that fellow the false Messiah – because the Truth of God is not in them, and the way of destruction is that "chosen" path of life.

 All this will transpire, for natural man, because he never accepted that Jesus was the true Messiah.

Even if you are yet a non-believer, or have fallen away from the church, there is still time to receive Jesus the real Messiah, for he still lives *within us* - and the truth is only in him.

Christ as Savior

God the Father loved the world so much that, as He knew mankind needed a Savior, Jesus came from heaven to walk with us, here on Earth, because he had a will to do so; in John 3:16, Scripture tells us that, "For God so love the world, that he gave his only begotten Son, that whosoever believeth in him should not perish, but have everlasting life" (John 3:16, KJV)

In my experience with Jesus, I lie not about what I have heard with my ears and saw with my eyes; these supernatural references are real, and I am here to say he is still alive, for His presence has his changed my life and I am writing this book to let you know Jesus exists, Jesus has spoken, and He is alive

The Book of Revelation, verse 1:18 states, "I am he that liveth, and was dead; and, behold, I am alive for evermore, amen; and have the keys of hell and of death" (Rev. 1:18, KJV); in other words, Jesus is telling us that He has all power and His is an awesome word.

Our acceptance of that has helped me to see clearly what the Lord has done in my life, the many things which the naked eye cannot see, unless God show you these supernatural things that I am able to write today.

When he made me his messenger, he did so, knowing that I would one day write a book like this for the many lost souls who do not yet know him – reminding them that Jesus is the true Son of God and that is not yet too late to accept Him as Lord and Savior.

While many out there may dismiss this by saying, "That's your religious belief," what the Lord has shown me, I speak not as some manmade religious tradition may act out, not having a true vision of who God really is and manipulating the Bible to fit their own purposes. They do this because they cannot yet see that the words contained within the Bible and the wisdom of the Scriptures are spirit and life – and that the only key to helping us understand how God truly works.

Thereby, I am not making this up – like many religions might do – as I speak only the truth and God know he has shown me many things so I am able to witness to Him and His truth.

Like I said and I say it again boldly Jesus Christ is the son of God who he has sent to be the savior to those who believe in him.

CHAPTER 9 - ALTAR CALL

Now, with everything laid on the table, in front of you, you have reached a point where you are asked to make the greatest decision you will make in your entire life – which is this: Where do you want to spend eternity at?

Many people tell me that they are not ready; when they do this, I like to ask them, "What better time is there, to give your life to the Lord? It has been set up for a special moment, your finding a personal connection with Him and recognizing the opportunity He set up for you to join Him and spend your eternal life in Heaven, having died for your sins on the cross so that you might be saved.

Those who fail believe in Him, even with the evidence laid before them, will not receive that salvation.

The things which cause people to say they are not ready – or which delay their decision, finding a church home, committing their lives to Him, and more – are doing so because they have succumbed to the evil spirits sent into this world to stop them.

Natural man is in trouble because he doesn't know the things of God because they are foolish to him. There are many people in this world, who are walking on thin ice and living a Russian roulette-type of existence, in which they take too many chances and foolish ventures, not knowing how they will affect tomorrow, just to get by – and continue on this path until it catches up with them, because they can only skirt hazards for so long until reality and their responsibilities to themselves and others catch up with them. When the day comes and their life is on the line – oh, watch out! – for death is a spirit which can hit you suddenly and grab ahold of you, and there will then be a battle over your spirit because darkness wants your soul, badly (and you are allowing that to happen because you are gambling over your life's decisions and where you will choose to spend eternity, each day that you live.)

There will be many who will say on, the Day of Judgment, "If only I would have received Jesus, when I had the chance" – but you do not have to be among that number, if you receive him *now*, as your Lord and personal Savior.

In Hebrews 3:15, Paul writes, "While it is said, today, if you will hear his voice, harden not your hearts, as in the provocation" (Heb. 3:15, KJV); s what he is telling us, here, is that it is important not to reject what is good for us.

When you find yourself wavering about a decision to follow Jesus, consider His commitment to you, as he has already loved you so much that He died on the cross for your sins, so that you can have eternal life with him. And if you have fallen away from Him, like the prodigal son (reference), now is the time to come back to the Lord.

Welcoming Jesus

I like to say, this is no joke people are dying every day not getting born again like someone as you; but all of a sudden you can make a change. It boils down to your commitment in walking with Him and living in His grace.

If you are serious in taking this next step, close your eyes, draw your breath, and pray:

"Lord Jesus, I am calling on Your name.
I believe, in my heart, that Jesus Christ is the Son of God.
I believe He die on the cross for all my sins.
I believe He rose the third day.
Thank you, Jesus, for living inside of me, from this day forth.
Amen"

By saying this prayer, your spirit will be *born again* – for, as the word of God tells us, in the second Book of Corinthians, chapter 5:17: "Therefore, if any man be in Christ, he is a new creature: old things are passed away; behold, all things are become new" (2 Cor. 5:17, KJV).

That is good if you truly meant it, from your heart – for you are child of God.

You can find affirmation, also, in Luke 15:10, which states, "I say unto you, there is joy in the presence of the angels of God over one sinner that repenteth" (Luke 15:10, KJV).

And, as Romans 10:9-13, we are told:

"That if thou shalt confess with thy mouth the Lord Jesus, and shalt believe in thine heart that God hath raised him, from the dead, thou shalt be saved. For with the heart man believeth unto righteousness; and with the mouth confession is made unto salvation. For the scripture saith, 'Whosoever believeth on him shall not be ashamed. For there is no difference between the Jew and the Greek: for the same Lord over all is rich unto all that call upon him. For whosoever shall call upon the name of the Lord shall be saved'" (Rom 10:9-13, KJV).

I am so joyful you made this choice – and it is important not to stop at this point, but to keep striving for the blessings that come from knowing God and Christ as Lord – and to let that faith lead you into a church that is fully of him: "Seek you first the kingdom of God, and his righteousness; and all these things shall be added unto you" (Mat. 6:33, KJV).

Remember: God has his way of doing things. And he will bless you as he promises; because God mean what he say and say what he means. Amen.

CHAPTER 10 - BEING BAPTIZED

The book of John goes in depth into the ministry of John the Baptist where, at the Jordan River, he baptized the people with water unto repentance.

This very baptism was the gateway for Jesus to come and get baptized. It is just as well for those who believe in Him to do the same, as, in laying down this path, Jesus lead by example in its significance in showing a commitment and the rebirth of the spirit that happens when we accept God and his mission in our lives.

There is no confusion from Jesus about the importance of baptism in a believer's life; the only grey areas there are, provide caution about the misunderstandings that can come across about how and when that baptism should happen.

In Matthew 28:18-20, Matthew recounts:

> "And Jesus came and spake unto them, 'All power is given unto me in heaven and in earth. Go you therefore, and teach all nations, baptizing them in the name of the Father, and of the Son, and of the Holy Ghost: Teaching them to observe all things whatsoever I have commanded you: and, lo, I am with you always, even unto the end of the world" (Matt. 28:18-20, KJV)

Amen.

It is important to hold on and not jump over the fence, just yet – for there is more revelation to these three verses than you can know. People have read these verses for years; and Churches of different denominations have been in strife and anger – or even just kept silent – on how to be baptized, even with these words from the Lord, which were to go forth and teach all nations about the importance of baptism.

This call was for the up-and-coming churches, from generation to generation.

Remember: Jesus has giving us the understanding in the book of Acts, as the first church follower in these baptisms.

It is important to remember that baptizing and being reborn with the Spirit of Christ removes the shroud of mystery that prevents you from understanding God and knowing Him, and the truths of living in His grace. The rules of the kingdom.

Jesus is quoted, in Mark 4:11, saying, "'Unto you it is given to know the mystery of the kingdom of God: but unto them that are without, all these things are done in parables" (Mark 4:11, KJV); this verse, itself, can be confusing – but we can take it to mean that, unless we accept all of the tenets of the Bible and the evidence presented to us in Scripture, we are blind to its greater meaning, and we cannot just take it piecemeal or consume only that which sounds good to us.

Baptism and its significance

Consider the three names which are given to us, to describe the nature of our living God, in Matthew 28:19: The Father, the Son, and the Holy Ghost.

When Jesus was describing the subject of baptism, he was talking about three different baptisms: baptism of the Father, baptism in Jesus' name, and baptism in the name of the Holy Spirit.

Baptism of the Father

The first baptizing is of the Father, which is repentance – and can sometimes be overlooked as a baptism. We can remember that John the Baptist performed a baptism of repentance, as part of his ministry, telling those who came to him at the Jordan River that they must reject the past and believe on what was to come.)

While significant, this baptism, alone, is incomplete – for it comes from repentance, as Jesus had not yet died on the cross, to pay that price (and the Holy Spirit was not yet released.) And it is John's baptism is still practice in many churches, when there are really two others – which Jesus also explained – and which must take place, within our faith.

Now, as someone has repented and believe in their heart that Jesus is the Son of God, their spirit gets born again and God now dwells within him (and he in God.) This happens by this confession, the Spirit of God being within you (as in 1-John 4:15) – but this is not the baptism of the Holy Spirit, which is a different component.

Baptism of the Son

This baptism, in Jesus name, occurs when a person submerges their entire body into water – not a sprinkle of water on you, as a symbol, but what is given us in the Greek word, *sozo*, which means to dip or submerge. (This appears in the original version of the New Testament, written in Greek.)

That's why it's always scriptures to back up how people receive water baptizing in Acts 10:48 Peter commanded them to be baptized in the name of the Lord which is Jesus, also in Acts 19:5 Apostle Paul went to Ephesus and water baptized some believers in Jesus Name. Just to remind you if we do everything in his name what's the problem of water baptizing all believers in his name, the Apostle did it in Acts and they were the first Church to show the rope for the up and coming churches. The number one reason why is because of religion errors, the Churches today should be following them in Acts on how to baptized, and they continuing daily with one accord and saw the supernatural without the division of religious names.

It is when we take away these divisions, we can be baptized and live in fellowship through Jesus and together as a church – and know the supernatural, as it appears in the book of Acts:

"But there was a certain man, called Simon, which beforetime in the same city used sorcery, and bewitched the people of Samaria, giving out that himself was some great one: To whom they all gave heed, from the least to the greatest, saying, 'This man is the great power of God. And to him they had regard, because that of long time he had bewitched them with the sorceries.' But when they believed Philip preaching the things concerning the kingdom of God, and the name of Jesus Christ, they were baptized, both men and women. Then Simon himself believed also: and when he was baptized, he continued with Philip, and wondered, beholding the miracles and signs which were done" (Acts 8:9-13, KJV)

Baptism of the Holy Spirit

This baptism is different from the other two, yet again, illustrated by Jesus in Acts 1:5 when he tells his disciples, "For John truly baptized with water; but ye shall be baptized with the Holy Ghost not many days hence" (Acts 1:5 , KJV).

Here, Jesus calls the Holy Spirit a baptism – recalled in what transpires in Acts 2:4, when "they were all filled with the Holy Ghost and began to speak in tongues, as the Spirit gave them the utterance" (Acts 2:4, KJV).

An incomplete baptism misses all of these important tenets, needed to be properly born again and be granted salvation – and given the keys to understanding God's commandments and presence in our lives, as believers.

We are cautioned against this in Acts 8:14-17, when the believer only had water baptized in Jesus name , they sent forth Peter and John notice this: they prayed for them that they might receive the Holy Ghost because the Spirit never has fallen on them, so they laid their hands on them and they receive the Holy Ghost:

"Now when the apostles which were at Jerusalem heard that Samaria had received the word of God, they sent unto them Peter and John: Who, when they were come down, prayed for them, that they might receive the Holy Ghost: (For as yet he was fallen upon none of them: only they were baptized in the name of the Lord Jesus.) Then laid they their hands on them, and they received the Holy Ghost" (Acts 8:14-17, KJV).

That goes to tell you that the Holy Spirit is not in everyone, unless the action of being baptized in the Spirit takes place.

I have heard it quite often, "But I already have the Holy Spirit in me."

However, if this has not happened according to the word of God, and in His righteousness, it's not in you – and you have been deceived by someone else, of even yourself. It is something which our religions and divisions among us have made it hard to understand, because they feel a need to use baptism in their own separate ways, for entry into church membership or even just for repentance – without recognizing the full significance of it, as outlined by Jesus in the New Testament for his believers. (Remember, again, as he died to redeem us for our sins and give us eternal life, we are now to be baptized in him and that Holy Spirit.)

We cannot fall back into traps about baptism and accept only one part of it, as cautioned in Luke 7:13: A man's incorrect beliefs can hold him back from the Truth.

Similarly, salvation cannot be bought, as when Simon – asked to buy the wisdom and power of the apostles so that he could lay hands and heal on his own, failing to see the larger picture (in Acts 8:18-19, KJV).

Now, the hour has come to take off the blindfolds and see through your eyes and not with them, We need to see that God is not holding back the truth, he is just waiting on us to obey what he has to say, to be born again and to walk with Him.

Amen.

Study scriptures

Galatians 2:20 KJV- I am crucified with Christ: nevertheless I live; yet not I, but Christ liveth in me: and the life which I now live in the flesh, I live by the faith of the Son of God, who loved me, and gave himself for me.

Ephesians 3:20 KJV- Now unto him that is able to do exceeding abundantly above all that we ask or think, according to the power that worketh in us.

Proverbs 3:5 thru 7 KJV- Trust in the Lord with all thine heart; and lean not unto thine own understanding. Verse 6, In all thy ways acknowledge him, and he shall direct thy paths. Verse 7, Be not wise in thine own eyes; fear the Lord, and depart from evil.

Romans 1:17 KJV- For therein is the righteousness of God revealed from faith to faith: as it is written, the just shall live by faith.

Romans 8:37 thru 39 KJV- Nay , in all these things we are more than conquerors through him that loved us. Verse 38, For I am persuaded, that neither death, nor life, nor angels, nor principalities, nor powers, nor things present, nor things to come. Verse 39, Nor depth, nor any other creature, shall be able to separate us from the love of God, which is in Christ Jesus our Lord.

1-Peter 5:6 thru 8 KJV- Humble yourselves therefore under the mighty hand of God, that he may exalt you in due time. Verse 7, Casting all your care upon him; for he careth for you. Verse 8, Be sober, be vigilant; because your adversary the devil, as a roaring lion, walketh about, seeking whom he may devour:

 Luke 4:4 KJV- And Jesus answered him, saying, it is written that man shall not live by bread alone, but by every word of God.

Luke 10:19 KJV- Behold, I give unto you power to tread on serpents and scorpions, and over all the power of the enemy: and nothing shall by any means hurt you.

1-Corinthians 10:13 KJV- There hath no temptation taken you but such as is common to man: but God is faithful, who will not suffer you to be tempted above that you are able; but will with the temptation also make a way to escape, that you may be able to bear it.

Isaiah 40:31 KJV- But they that wait upon the Lord shall renew their strength; they shall run, and not be weary; and they shall walk and not faint.

Galatians 5:22 thru 23 KJV- But the fruit of the Spirit is love, joy, peace, longsuffering, gentleness, goodness, faith. Verse 23, Meekness, temperance: against such there is no law.

Philippians 4:13 KJV- I can do all through Christ which strengtheneth me.

Philippians 4:6 thru 8 KJV- Be careful for nothing; but in every thing by prayer and supplication with thanksgiving let your requests be made known unto God. Verse 7, And the peace of God, which passeth all understanding, shall keep your hearts and minds through Christ Jesus. Verse 8, Finally, brethren, whatsoever things are true, whatsoever things are honest, whatsoever things are just, whatsoever things are lovely, whatsoever things are of good report; if there be any virtue, and if there be any praise, think on these things.

Ephesians 6:10 thru 13 KJV- Finally, my brethren, be strong in the Lord, and in the power of his might. Verse 11, Put on the whole armour of God, that ye may be able to stand against the wiles of the devil. Verse 12, For we wrestle not against flesh and blood, but against principalities, against powers, against the rulers of the darkness of this world, against spiritual wickedness in high places. Verse 13,

Wherefore take unto you the whole armour of God, that ye may be able to withstand in the evil day, and having done all, to stand.

Made in the USA
Monee, IL
04 January 2022

86880516R00017